Quicksand

poems by

S. J. Stephens

Finishing Line Press
Georgetown, Kentucky

Quicksand

Copyright © 2023 by S. J. Stephens
ISBN 979-8-88838-267-7 First Edition
All rights reserved under International and Pan-American Copyright Conventions. No part of this book may be reproduced in any manner whatsoever without written permission from the publisher, except in the case of brief quotations embodied in critical articles and reviews.

ACKNOWLEDGMENTS

Literary Journals & Magazines:
"Elegy Written to my Younger Self," *Crepe and Penn Quarterly*
"I Open the Door to You at 3am," *Scapegoat Review*
"Self-Portrait of Flesh and Bone," *Insideout, an Affirming Epiphany,* Greater Cincinnati Artists
"The Irreversibility of Rain;" "In Love with Your Ghosts;" "An Ordinary Evening;" "Pretty Smiles;" "Seven Bends the Road to Seven;" "Lie with Me in This Moment;" "Quicksand;" "Hang Me in The Louvre" *Adelaide Literary Magazine*
"90's Girl," *Writing in a Woman's Voice*
"My Tangled Hair," *Garfield Lake Review*

Publisher: Leah Huete de Maines
Editor: Christen Kincaid
Cover Art and Design: Shari G. Rust
Author Photo: S. J. Stephens

Order online: www.finishinglinepress.com
also available on amazon.com

Author inquiries and mail orders:
Finishing Line Press
PO Box 1626
Georgetown, Kentucky 40324
USA

Table of Contents

I

Quicksand 1

lie with me in this moment 2

Handfuls of Light 3

Erase the Broken Things 4

The Tax I Pay 5

Elegy Written to My Younger Self 6

Blue Eye-Shadow: A Soundtrack to the 90's 8

Little Deaths After a Twenty-sixth Birthday Party 10

Self-Portrait of Flesh and Bone 11

Waiting for the Hours to Change 12

All These Verbs to Catch an End 13

Dear Child, I Dream 14

Pretty Smiles 15

II

Hang Me in the Louvre 19

I Open the Door to You at 3AM 20

My Tangled Hair 21

The Irreversibility of Rain 22

Flower's Elegy, 2006 23

Straight Girl Crush 24

I'd Build a House of this Moment 25

You Have Taken the World I Was 26

Release Me Softly 27

An Ordinary Evening 28

My Scrumptious Twinkie, A Parody 29

Eutrophication 30

Broken Wings 31

In Love with Your Ghost 32

I

Quicksand

I open the door to my house and fall slowly,
slowly, I am pulled under into social media quicksand
where the free exchange of ideas should flourish. I find
a wasteland swallows me, swallows me whole with words
that find and feed suppressed hate and judgements
I wish were no longer part of our make-up. We create
fictionalized personas who forget—

Anger feels good but cultivates little else.

In this glass house with broken windows
scattered on the floor, we forget the most basic
principles of peace—

Darkness cannot drive out darkness.

We have the dignity to clear shadows of politics, opinion and race,
instead we are pulled under, we suffocate in apathy, turn black
and blue in the viscosity of this beast, where peaceful protests
become riots and friends become enemies, where the darkness
covers our eyes and we miss—

Unique and beautiful differences that make us whole.

We need only turn on the light, open the window, throw
a rope into the quicksand, pull free basic humanity and see—
black and white are not the grains of sand pulling us under.
God, religion, sexual orientation, gender, do not generate hate,
these labels do not divide us, we are divided by judgement
by stereotypes, by words and actions that don't follow
the basic tenets of humanity—

Love thy neighbor… do unto others… speak from love.

lie with me in this moment

                                        sink into the book of me
where all my stories wait to be told. Take out the pages
and read—

It's not quite Spring here, where Winter lags in the heat
and humidity of our bodies in this haven,
the open waiting universe where I want you to escape

with me, defeat darkness and demons, they will penetrate
our humanness. I tell you—
                      All my demons are on the inside.

You know I believe in both heaven and hell—this hell, time spent
fighting the current toward the winter solstice, where I mark the light
with fingers in the air, ticking the time—tilting to the highest

point of daylight—*That's no way to live* you say, when burying
your fingers into my sense of time and space. Waiting
is death—drowning in the time between reveling and wrangling

spirits, in the chasm of skin and sinew and organ and cell. I want
to plunge into these stories, learn secrets, translate the meaning—
                    in a way you can understand.

I ask you again, to lie with me—I've opened
the book to the page I hope you peruse with delicate
fingers, fathom this craving to be felt outside a passionate

embrace. I hunger for the taste of being known, intimately
not chastely, not romantically, not by the flush of skin we've
already tasted. In this space I lift the impregnable veil between

who I am and who I appear to be, who you want me
to be and who I fear I am. All this to say—
I need to be seen.

Handfuls of Light

Blue sky meets the blue sea in the distance
it sings against the shore where I sit and drag

my fingers through the sand, mining for rapture,
the wind whisks salt into my hair, against

my lips and skin, I'm sticky as if drenched in sugar,
Reaching to the sky to release sorrow

I catch handfuls of light,
mistake them for a blessing

While warmth escapes through my fingertips
I wait for turtles to descend from the sea

to watch them plant babies in the marsh—
carry tradition to the next generation

Waiting for the spirit of blessing to find me
I need to be filled by the sacred

I need those turtles to come
to witness some kind of birth.

Erase the Broken Things

The troubadour of broken things
plays havoc with my veins
beats a drum to deafen pretty dreams.

I too take my waking slow. Like embers
graying beneath the morning dew.
When I blow, the song bursts

lighting morning, igniting chords
that needle low in my spine.
A woeful beating, to sow what's left

of sleep deep into my body, where
I carry it with me. The pills I swallow are
an ode to the aching I bellow, as I would

a love song. The tingling of sleep in my limbs
a deadening, anesthesia to my pain,
numbing memories of my lover, they choke

life from all I've planted, he
is the overgrown and neglected plot.
We swell with need to be plucked

and loved well. Left to dry in the sun
streaming through the blinds, it bathes me alone
in bed, with need to erase broken things.

The Tax I Pay

Perhaps God forgot to give me light
          when I laid in my mother's womb,
      maybe it washed away through the placenta
        like water down the drain.

Perhaps I was here to suffer
          the way a dog buries his bone, or
      I let that bone be buried in me to ward off the dark
        I can't otherwise escape.

Perhaps when I slipped from my mother's body
          the moon pooled on the floor with her blood.
    it left a peace that must be fed
        from the breast of humanity.

Perhaps I lost that humanness somewhere
          between her womb and today, and
    the only song inside me turns sour
        when I cut my flesh to sing, or

Perhaps its red that runs from the razor sharp streaks
          marked on my flesh
    Perhaps when I bleed it is penance,
        the tax I pay with pain.

Elegy Written to My Younger Self

I didn't realize
bikes were different for boys and girls

So, I broke my hymen
on an old rusty hand-me-down Schwinn

Racing the neighbor kid, I hit a rock, sprang
forward on the crossbar, and tore the thin red membrane

At eight years old I had no names for Female parts
but I won that race and held the rights

to neighborhood bragging the rest of the summer

                                                  Later that year

I had a series of urinary tract infections
the doctor examined my down there with worry

asked my mother if anyone abused me
I remember the visit, the embarrassment

mother's concern, and a child's bewilderment

                                                  That same year

my brother impregnated his 16-year old girlfriend
So, I asked my mother how babies grow

She brought out a book to show
the stages of development

I learned words like vagina and uterus, placenta
and ovum, and before I understood

what they were, I hated the word
vulva. If someone told me what I'd discover

I would have kept my curiosity at bay

                     A few years later, at the Library

the neighborhood boys found the *Joy of Sex*
showed me a sketch of a man's hairy penis

from that moment on I couldn't stand
to be hugged by my Dad, and when my teenage

years brought crushes; I relished the unrequited
distance between myself and
                                      all those penises

Blue Eye-Shadow: A Soundtrack to the 90's

I wanted to be Madonna—with her stacked jelly bracelets and forbidden sexuality—a style of every nineties girl's dream and every boy's fantasy—she was more than ambition mocking virginity and scoffing the doctrine of her youth—daring to defy the laws of man and church—In my room singing—*La Isla Bonita*—with little idea of its meaning—*A young girl with eyes like the desert*—the music moved through my body—sang to my innocence at the first mention of wild dreams and tropical storms gathering inside—I was touched beneath my skin—through my bones—into the marrow—where all secrets held—wait

        It was a time of designer Guess jeans and peg rolled pants—high ponytails—and that guy who believed I was—*on fire for the lord*—and—I was burning in that fire—deeply immersed in the word—but also submerged in Bel Biv Devoe—*Do Me Baby* and—Color me Bad—*I Wanna Sex You Up*—Boys to Men singing—*I'll Make Love To You*

        My first kiss—a dead thing flopping on wet sand—before love—came with a second kiss—and his hand covering my breast—kneading my flesh—a deafening music—tuned to perfection—but boys make lousy lovers on driveways—with clumsy attempts at seduction—even when the stars are clear—warm summer air cooled by the hour—submerged in feeling—under a spell that resonates through decades of good lovers—and bad lovers—beneath those first moments of bliss—when rational thought lost—to the hum of lust—I want that magic in every kiss in every touch of lips—and—in my lover's words

We were—pretty girls with blue eyeshadow and black mascara—pink cheeks and frosted pink lips—teased hair three inches high—and hairspray stuck to the bathroom floor—we were girls on the verge—before cell phones and computers—a dark craze emerged—Madonna posed naked on the street—pushing the limits of virtue—beyond what my experience could beat out in time to the righteous music playing in the background—a soundtrack to the nineties

After rock n roll—Ruth Bader Ginsberg and Madeleine Albright—gave way to the commercialization of my body—tricked into objectifying my sex—until—we—all women—bleed openly—reduced to sexuality—stripped of power—we slit our own wrists—in unwitted suicide

        I fear that legacy as I am the nineties girl living proof that progress isn't always progress—my misspent regrets are worthless in the currency of living—pennies on the dollar in the exchange of memories at today's rate—I'll keep my memories—because I know this wild ride isn't new   every generation—lives through decades of change—and at least I know—while you   exploited my girlhood—

        I am an unapologetic bad ass feminist.

Little Deaths After a Twenty-sixth Birthday Party

There is only silence in a red
dress lying ripped on the floor,
the stain of breath rendering
my body useless, plucking apple
blossoms, blood brushed tips
open in full blush—coarse
fingers dipped in murder,
from the apex of full thighs,
bruises of winter budding
grief, it flourishes dark,
rough indifference
the way a treehouse is blown
down in a bellowing wind.

Self-Portrait of Flesh and Bone

> *Dedicated to the artist who shared his self-portrait as an act*
> *Of self-acceptance, and in hope that his art would be a healing.*

We asked you to apply paint to your skin
the way Van Gogh painted *Starry Nights*,
Impasto—visible, with thickly textured strokes
      but you were bold, and found your own form.
Absorbed in calibrating each identity to fit tight,
we blindly offer you a perfectly constructed puzzle,
the kind we laminate and hang on the wall
as we would your self-portrait.
      Your self-portrait, a calling-card of flesh and bone
      scraped with a palette knife's precision
      to leave only one hungry, impassioned eye open.
We can see how pain and passion grow like a vine
climbing past conventional doctrine
that commands you to conform.

      You've taken our command and refuse to conform,
      standing with your vine, allowing yourself to grow
      beyond the brush's embrace, letting go
      all you inherit, all we impose in favor of shaping your own
            mystery. Let us know you alone own
            this story, the experience of brush strokes
            left visible on your skin, as time wakes
            you to understanding and growth within
      yourself. Celebrate living inside a body
      that doesn't dictate who you are or what you desire,
      how you should feel and how you should attire
      perception of your humanness—or community.
Hold strong dear friend, dear brave human, lovely soul,
Make us take notice of you, yourself who is unique and individual.

Waiting for the Hours to Change

The taste of your strawberry wine dallies
in my mouth. The delicate skin you peeled
left the sweetest meat, plump and juicy
and tender where my teeth extract flavor.
Our bodies gambol as I add up the minutes,
the seconds hovering toward two am.
Our existence becomes a pause as the clock
changes its ticking. We plunge past a halted
hour, and what's lost, is lost to us.
When we wake your taste is still as sweet
and you're captured in my mettle, ripe
with what's left unsaid.
I want to cherish all that is caught,
all that's forgotten in the epoch.

Verbs to Catch an End

Free a glimmer of hope,
fill it with bones, and
hang it from the breast,
balancing the blistering sun
lassoed to my tears and
buckled to well-thumbed news,
burn this house down with the
strike of words against stone,
seize broken talk between the
latched lips of distance, know in
gathering each other's voices, we
arrest all this unrest among us, make us
clutch the skin, language, living we
rope together in a collage, time to
grasp the weeds with all hands
clasped in unison, in unity we
clip away the inches, slowly,
becoming one is simple this way,
hooking love to flapping tongues
ensnares today with possibility, if we
clutch together, it ends.

Dear Child, I Dream

I dream of and for you, see my mother
in the curve of your cheek, in eyes that slice
through the stormy ocean of my own.
Knowing you inherit all that exists between
San Marco Island, Italy and Elk Valley, Tennessee
my wishes rain, they penetrate you
down to the marrow, there your father
lives only in DNA. In my sleep
I dream the silhouette of you
as the visible orb of a daylight moon,
it sutures my body where I'm cracked,
where I bleed for you, your life,
your living. You're an unhealed wound
even medicine cannot cure.

I wake to a chest full of fool's gold,
feed the idea of you until you grow
and flower, a blossom I could pluck
before you become a shadow of leaves
lost, like dried prunes. You hold
my dreaming of you inside your cells,
formed inside my mother before
you could form in seedlings
I planted deep in unfertile
soil, deep in pots and planters
I store in the garage.

Pretty Smiles

Don't place your arm around my neck
I've been taught to accommodate your
ego at the expense of my own. Don't put your
hand on my arm as if I need comfort, your fake
attentions. Don't tell me I'd be prettier if I'd smile,
my teeth are razer-sharp utensils I use to cut
you open, gut the patriarchy and condescension out
of your doctrine with a salacious chuckle.
Don't tell me my smile is lovely as if my lips
were red delicious, they'll bleed when you sink
your teeth into my juicy skin. Don't lick,
the blue from my eyes for your own glories.
Step in, peel the tattered layers and discover my furies
expose my luscious female flesh, it will, be scandalous.

II

Hang Me in the Louvre

I don't want a portrait that creates
a static moment in time. If
it was 1910, and I his muse,
I'd ask Pablo to paint me like Gertrude
reduce me to mass on his canvas,
what he observed in his avant-garde fashion.
I'd ask him to deconstruct me, reassemble
me, make me visible through fragmented perception.
I'd ask him to paint me in hues of gravity
in cubist style of his *Girl with a Mandolin*,
break me down to geometrical elements,
develop a new comprehension
of the unabridged inner chaos I suffer,
when in deep, deep depression.

In the time before he returned to neoclassicism,
I'd like to hang on the wall of the Louvre,
nails driven through my frame,
curving and warping the space,
hanging beside his other women. I'd ask Pablo
to teach me how to see through his artist's eye
and experience the movement of his brushstroke,
brown to pale to beige and the blue-green
of my eyes, juxtapose the dark planes, smooth
my rugged cheek, imbue my flesh with plasticity,
the dissolution of my essence on the page,
until I am recognizable, only as color and shape.

I Open the Door to You at 3AM
Inspired by Meg Day

It's Saturday— I say with a sultry gasp
the only chant whose chorus we remember—
you reach for me like I was another woman
until you remember, only with me, in my arms
do you resonate in silence as you do in sound.
A shaft of pale moon reaches me, I turn to you
in the shadow we draw on the wall. These layered
covers, where our bodies plummet
and resurface—wistful coins in the fountain
of kings, your chest bobbing bronze and even
as you move against cobalt sheets. It devastates
me, the grinding of the springs when you crawl
into darkness, drag it over our bodies.
Your eyes, stars—gleaming from the dark
where I throb below and am drenched
in pulsations your pelvis yields. Sustain me
in this place of miniscule warmth that nips
at the edge of some altered existence.
You could listen while I exhale: a golden echo
like a comet passing this planet in
twilight. You conceive once more of spinning
in this echelon and materialize here
when I summon in a tone only your engorged
ego might recognize. Don't abandon me, not this me—
cradled, claiming all the echoes of ecstasy
existed within a lyric known and sung.
I watch the speckle of coarsely toothed shapes
on the wall while the shades cut in a slight
breeze, exodus leaves me dry as a licked dog bone
until another 3am recovers this melody.

My Tangled Hair

You told me once I have sex hair
while you played me that song,
the one with people chanting their religion.
You tangled your fingers in my hair
when you rolled toward me, pressed
your body to mine, before your kiss hijacked
my memories. Your fingers remain entwined
in my hair, always tangled when I see you sing
on stage at York Street Café
when your eyes watch me lean in
to the remembered affection.
You could have been the sun, you could play
at the center, instead, like Pluto on the outer rim
of the universe, you watched planets spin

while you snarled your fingers in my hair. In
your apartment you said *I love the reflection
of me in your eyes*, and what a waste
the connection would be if I turned on the light
to that moment, that important view of you
in my eyes, it spilled unspoken heat. Who
cleaned it off the floor where you took that
kiss? It was more than a moment
treasured, a moment coveted, as you weaved
your fingers through my hair. You walked
home to live in the easy, where you are contented.
I can only wish you were brave enough to be happy
to leap off the moon, to catch me,
courage wasn't in your appeal,
it wasn't in your landscape to come to me, yet
you remain, entangled.

The Irreversibility of Rain
Inspired by Victoria Chang

Sarah died violently on February 12, 2012 at half past noon on a rainy Monday in a busy shopping mall parking lot, canoodled in the front seat of her car when the words I need to take a break struck her chest like the sound of metal penetrating wood when a nail gun releases its momentum. The shadow of raindrops covered her lover when she looked up from her death rattle, a last breath of light shone from her open mouth like a beacon of poison before it pressed closed, the way lips do in an absent minded kiss. She was laid to rest in a burial of I love yous with all her things tightly tied in a plastic grocery bag, knotted so that nothing of her would escape, so that nothing of her would be left behind. When someone dies alone in a car, memories are the last words she hears in the silent heaviness of rain slapping the windshield.

Flower's Elegy, 2006

The purple painted roses arrived
post mortem, petals browning.
I put them in a vase to remind me
of slow days on the beach when you
took my hand, professed my beauty
and I believed. Purple dust settled
on the counter before I could press
the petals for safe keeping. Stems
hardened and stood as small soldiers
guarding sentiment, guarding things
I didn't say, knowing all the pieces
pitched in the trash would bleed
from thorns, they tore at my fingers
until shreds of you hung from the tips,
swayed to the song you wrote about
my eyes, my right hand still bears scars.
I wasn't ready to understand intimate
nights aren't meant to ache, aren't meant
to leave wounds. You told me you almost
loved me, and that it should count,
But maybe you meant you did love me
and I clasped the dried petals into dust
as they slipped through my fingers
landed in a herbaceous border where
blossoms eventually fade.

Straight Girl Crush

You have a secret loveliness I want to scoop out
and interrogate, look at under a microscope, break down
into elements, cells, atoms, subatomic particles,
until I can distill your essence and absorb it.

How exquisite you speak, you move me, tilt me off axis, change my
direction. I am struck, transformed.
How generous you are with your voice, it resonates
line, language, and metaphor, they *are muscular.*

I can feel those words with my tongue,
a remora eating scraps of your power,
forming a symbiotic bond where we master
the decadence of language.

When I sneak out my own door, can I sink into yours,
mingle with your species, be gobies and shrimp on the ocean floor?
Guide me out of blindness, create a safe space. Your eyes
a sonnet, an enchantment, an obsessive moment.

I long to hear what happens in the silence between
your melody and thoughts in the lilt of your delicate fingers.
Whatever your truth costs I will pay and be made sharper, push the
devastation into me, I will revel in fascination.

You are a virtuoso of creation to behold, a noun
I want to become—an embodied, breathing possession.

I'd Build a House of this Moment

I want to lie on fine bones
as relaxed spoons in a drawer,
tightly fit silver untouched
as the unknown comfort
of two birds huddled in winter.
I gather in warmth, all my pieces
drain the damage, coalesce,
clotting to cover wounds, down
pillows me in a dead-armed embrace,
hips curve in where skin pursues
skin, fingers skim my bare spaced
frame, hair tousled on the pillow
with honeyed whispers,
I'd build a house of now
pinnacle this bed in the center,
where fires burn I sleep on divine
bones, phantom sighs lip my neck,
and there's no cost, no penalty to pay.

You Have Taken the World I Was
    Title from Anne Carson's "O Small Ecstasy of Love"

Steadfast in your siren arms, I worry
you might swing away from me on stars.
Take me with you in flight where there is only suicide,
and I will welcome the death of *the world I was.*

New, I will spin in your orbit, web in electrical wires,
in conduit you manipulate before you turn on the power.
If I break the light switches you installed,
this planet will burn down even as I revolve

around new energy, revel in your momentum.
You are with me here, circling the center
of this discovered universe.
We can't call it the sun, we would burn out,

no life can live so close to the center,
we'll stick to this new home we've constructed
and live in the growing embrace, feed
on morning hunger, mouths open to fill

our bellies with honeyed comets.

Release Me Softly

I crack open my chest, scoop out the contents
to gift wrap and lie at your feet. You fling
it aside like other unwanted, forgotten things.
It seeps from the edges, reminiscent
of a bruise gathering heat beneath skin,
as if it weren't a kind of madness,
like looking directly into the sun
blinds what's left of me with searing sadness.
Weeping rosebuds you gave me have died,
a crimson congregation now bowed
in prayer. I trace the edges, shriveled
blooms graze my lips- breathe in the scattered
petals. The forgotten and dead are buried
in me, grow a widow with arms soaked red.

I wear a black veil to the epigraph
where I kneel before the monument,
knowing this burial will cultivate
grief that reeks with a painful epitaph.
So, I take the prescribed pills that murder
thoughts, until this body wears like a coffin
weighted with a muted satisfaction
as Xanax flows through veins thick with offer-
ings of peace. My winter tongue drips with ice
that waters bones and lotus flowers, grows
damaged cerebellum, blurred vision slows
weaken muscles as I lie in distance.
Ataxia and dysarthria deliver
release, softly, from you whom I adore.

An Ordinary Evening

You string words together and whisper,
hoping the night has found me vulnerable,
lonely enough to surrender

to your spin the bottle seduction. An ordinary evening
on my couch, watching a movie, laughter
an aphrodisiac that plays me pliable

to the tantalizing touch of the brush
of your fingers in innocent places, the palm
of my hand, the slope of my shoulder, the curve

of my neck, you captivate me in common,
in the comfort of a moment
reserved for intimate nights when I forget

I hate you, when memories suspend
hurt hurdling towards morning,
I remember only the sublime, and spin.

My Scrumptious Twinkie, A Parody

After Harryette Mullen's "Dim Lady" and Shakespeare's Sonnet 130

My Sugar Lips' gaze is nothing like a blaze and Ohio mud is ruddier than his muzzle, his complexion less crimson than pale. If his perruque were corkscrews, then bronze noodles sprout from his dome in russet rings. I have seen mighty handsome lumber jacks with red and black flannel, but no such prince do I see in his face. I love to hear his bellow, yet I know his tune is off key more than Britney without auto-tune. And in some sweet wine celebration, there is more syrup in my baby's beer-tinged puff than any fragrant flower. I don't know any Achilles or Brad Pitt doppelgangers, my man is from top to bottom ordinary, and yet, by the love, my white chocolate Reese's cup has more allure than any hero of the silver screen whose pop-stardom status will soon dim.

Eutrophication
Inspired by Jericho Brown

Our passion began in intrigue, in believe,
left well-lived remains full of remedy, relived
in a sticky-fingered pendulum pitched forward,
a rare performance of movement. Heave
this eye, glossy and filled with days spent
writing songs, playing dungeons and dragons,
and planting Amaryllis lagoons.
We could swim in the blooms, stems bent
in reverence to the sweetest slippery taste
of scum thickening, cyanobacteria grow
these dead zones we won't see as we furrow.
We are caterpillars, Lily Borers active in heat.
We began, hungering, and leave tunneling
into leaves, we feed, cocoon, and swing.

Broken Wings

You came to me with broken wings
and hand grenades.
I wanted your healing, I wanted songs
after all these years of fractured promises
and damaged hearts—there are still
flowers in the vase. But the cat
knocked it off the counter.
I woke to the spill and splinter—
glass stuck, ripped the red
from all the joy I felt at the fresh
scent of Daisies, Hyacinth, and Alstroemeria.
All that beauty ended up in the trash.
Was it a loving gesture? Cat paws
swiping in play at the unfamiliar treasure.
Did the explosion come from my hands?
Every eruption of the last thirty years
rattles in the sweep of straw fingers
pushing pieces into the dust pan.
This ends the way everything
ends, in deafening sound
of screaming inside my head,
the rush of hormones overwhelming
the antidepressants I swallow to be balanced.
Is disease to blame for death or
is it the flowers lining the trash bin?

In Love with Your Ghost

Tonight, I follow the Ohio River—
driving south through West Virginia,
it winds into mountains, behind me.

where one hill curves around another
I write the words to every story inside me
onto dark Virginia roads.

I am captive to backseat ghost riders—
transparent bodies who refuse to be left behind.
These nights are dangerous, remembering dangerous.

Near midnight I can no longer hide and I reach
for ghosts where bodies lived—
I find the time a friend's boyfriend

molested me, she placed the blame
between my blades, it weights the luggage packed
neatly on the back seats.

I find the time my love and I held hands
at the Renaissance Fair with horns strapped
to our heads— auroras on the edge of Blue Ridge.

The more I ruminate on him—
the fonder I become, until
I'm more in love than when he existed.

Confined in my car, covered in diverted energy,
specters I no longer want frolic in the flares.
By 1 a. m., my eyelids at half mast, my vision

blurred by the light of streetlamps cast
on North Carolina roads
recklessness necklaced, stretched wide.

Near 2 a. m., my memories distill
become fresh blooms, fresh wounds—
fresh whispers in the dark.

S.J. Stephens lives with her Siamese cat, Khaleesi, and writes in the coastal town of Wilmington, NC. She has an MFA in poetry from the University of North Carolina, Wilmington; where she was the Managing Editor of *Chautauqua Literary Journal* for two years. As a transplant from Cincinnati, OH, she also holds a BA in Communications from the College of Mount St. Joseph and an MA in English from Northern Kentucky University. Stephens has published in a variety of journals including *Garfield Lake Review* and *the Sandy River Review,* was a 2020 Adelaide Literary Award Finalist, and her chapbook, *Where All the Birds Are Dancing*, was released in October 2020 by Finishing Line Press. Deeply influenced by the natural world and the beautiful landscapes of Cincinnati and Wilmington, it is her desire to write with the honesty, bravery, and humanity of other female poets.

www.ingramcontent.com/pod-product-compliance
Lightning Source LLC
Chambersburg PA
CBHW022124090426
42743CB00008B/1002